Introduction

Saintpaulia and Felis domesticus "Sunshine"

Saintpaulia 'Cradle Song'

Sinningia pusilla

Saintpaulia 'Superstar'

Artistic planting

In less than two generations, African violets have come out of the forests of Africa to become the most popular flowering houseplant in America. There are many reasons for their phenomenal attraction. The most obvious is the colorful profusion of flowers that frequently last for months. Another reason is the fact that they thrive in the same temperature and humidity ranges that are found in most homes. Furthermore, they are inexpensive and easily propagated.

Though the originals certainly were from Africa, African violets are not true violets. They were given this common name because of their violet-shaped flowers in various shades of blue.

Botanically, African violets are of the genus *Saintpaulia*. A genus (genera is the plural) is a classification of plants with common characteristics. It is the main subdivision of a family. *Saintpaulias*, for instance, are members of a larger family called Gesneriaceae. In addition to African violets, this group consists of at least 130 other genera and includes such popular houseplants as florist gloxinias and "lipstick plants." The non-African violets in this family are collectively referred to as "gesneriads."

In 1892, Baron von Saint Paul found and collected specimens of African violets in the forests of northeast Tanganyika (known today as Tanzania). He sent seeds to his father who turned them over to the Royal Botanic Gardens in Germany. The Director of the Gardens brought several plants to flower and realized that these were a new discovery. He named them *Saintpaulia ionantha* in honor of the man who found them. The second name indicates the species and means "with violet-like flowers." Soon, the African violet was grown and offered for sale by plant firms all over Europe.

In 1927, an American nursery imported some African violet seeds from England with the intention of producing new varieties. By 1936, after years of careful cross-breeding, ten superior hybrid varieties were developed and named. Led by the famous 'Blue Boy,' these plants found their way into millions of American homes. As their popularity increased, a demand for new and different African violets arose. The variety of plants we are able to buy today, are products of a handful of dedicated individuals known as hybridizers.

Where they come from

Photography courtesy of Tom Talpey

Gesneria pauciflora near a stream in Puerto Rico

The Green House, Bellflower, California

Today, African violets can still be found growing wild in the Usambara and Uluguru hills of eastern Africa. This part of Tanzania is heavily forested and is only eight degrees from the equator. The climate is tropical, with only two distinct seasons — hot and warm. Pockets of fallen leaves and moss beside the many streams and waterfalls provide the ideal home for approximately 20 natural species. They all have single flowers in various shades of blue and purple.

The humidity in the tropical forests is usually above 90 percent. Frequent warm showers are followed by hot sun. Thanks to tangled forests, the temperature in the shady glens seldom exceeds 90°F (32°C). In fact, the temperature rarely varies from night to day, season to season. The uniform temperatures are responsible for the absence of any discernable dormant state in African violets. Hybridizers have accomplished much in adapting today's African violets to home conditions.

Other gesneriads grow wild all over the world. With a few exceptions, they are mostly found in warm, tropical areas within 20 degrees of the equator. The greatest number of gesneriads come from Mexico, the West Indies, Central and South America. There are a few gesneriads that are hardy to winter weather. Called "alpines," they are native to Europe and Japan.

African violets are so popular, you can buy them from just about anyplace that sells plants. Garden centers, plant stores, florists, supermarkets and department stores have all been known to carry quality varieties. The largest and most varied selection of African violets is usually available from specialty nurseries and mail order businesses.

If you are personally selecting an African violet, it is worth the time to carefully examine it. Compare the plants and choose the one with the freshest and cleanest looking foliage. On single-crown plants, the leaves should grow in a symmetrical pattern. Check both sides of the leaves for signs of insects, spots, stains or discoloration.

A newly purchased African violet should always be handled with care. To avoid spreading insects and diseases, keep the new plant isolated from your other plants and observe it for a period of at least two weeks. Immediate heavy watering and direct sun should be avoided. Introduce it gradually to the optimum conditions recommended by the grower.

Another pleasant way to obtain African violets and gesneriads is to attend a local or regional show of such plants. Here you can meet other plant enthusiasts who are often willing to sell or swap seeds, leaf cuttings and plants. You can also find out about various clubs that may have chapters or affiliates in your neighborhood.

Natural characteristics

Fringed single   Multi-color double   Fringed double   Semi-double

Plain single   Single star   Fantasy   Double

African violet flowers

Longifolia   Plain or tailored   Ruffled   Holly   Quilted

Red-backed   Girl   Spooned   Variegated   Serrated

African violet leaves

The color of the African violet flower is derived from a group of pigments that are predominantly blue and pink. Therefore, even with cross-breeding, the majority of flowers are blue, purple or pink. If none of these pigments are present, the flower is white.

Hybridizers have managed to extend the limitations of the natural colors by producing two-toned flowers. A flower with a contrasting edge is known as a "Geneva." A rayed, streaked or splotched flower is called a "fantasy."

All African violet flowers have at least five petals. The typical arrangement is called a "single" and consists of two small upper petals and three larger lower petals. A pair of yellow pollen sacs, called "anthers," are conspicuous in the center of the flower.

One variation is called a "double." It is made up of the same flat circle of petals as a single, but an inner ring of tufted petals is present. These petals sometimes hide the anthers. A "semi-double" is similar to a double, but the tufted inner petals do not quite cover the anthers.

Star-shaped African violets differ from the above in that all five petals are the same size and are symmetrically arranged. Also available are fringed or ruffled flowers. These range from flowers with deeply tasseled edges to ones with just slight serrations on the petals.

Even the type of African violet foliage is varied. One of the earliest varieties introduced in America had a plain round leaf. Originally called "boy foliage," it is now referred to as "plain" or "tailored" foliage. When a mutated lack of chlorophyll produced a leaf with a yellow spot at the base, it was only natural that it be called "girl foliage."

Other types of foliage include quilted leaves (with distinctly raised areas between leaf veins), longifolia leaves (long, narrow and pointed), variegated leaves (green leaves with shading from light green and pink to cream), serrated leaves (with notched margins), ruffled leaves (with curled edges almost bordering on fringe), holly leaves (crested leaves resembling holly), spooned leaves (leaves that cup up along the sides), and red-backed leaves (with a dark red backing between the veins).

The leaves grow from the top part of the stem. This growing point is called a "crown." The stem below is the "neck." Occasionally, the crown will naturally develop additional growing points, called "suckers." If left alone, these are responsible for developing multiple-crowned plants.

Other gesneriads also include a wide range of foliage and flower shapes, colors and sizes. *Columneas* are trailing plants with unusual shaped flowers in bright reds and yellows. *Episcias* are grown for their exotically patterned foliage and brilliant red flowers.

Light and temperature

African violets in a bright, humid location

African violet as its own light meter

Too little light

Right light

Too much light

Gesneriad growing outside

African violets must have lots of light in order to produce flowers. In fact, African violets can usually take all the indirect light they can get most of the year. They can even tolerate occasional early morning or late afternoon direct sun, especially in spring, fall and winter. You will have to protect your plants from direct summer sun, as it is usually too intense. Too much light will burn the foliage, causing it to turn yellow.

Observing the plant is often the best way to determine how much light is sufficient. If the leaves become leggy with long stalks, they need more light. If the leaves curl downward and cup around the pot, they are getting too much light (a few varieties will naturally grow this way). If the leaves grow relatively flat, the light is satisfactory.

African violets can be grown near any well-lighted window. Any directional exposure is fine, although a western exposure is generally good all year. If you find that a single location is not good both winter and summer, do not hesitate to move your plants to another window.

Symmetry is important to the health and appearance of an African violet. To maintain this growth, all leaves must receive equal amounts of light. Each week, you should turn your plants a quarter turn in one direction. Crowding also limits light and spoils even growth. Your collection should be spaced so that the leaves do not touch.

Unlike many houseplants, African violets thrive in the same temperatures that most people find comfortable. The ideal is an even temperature close to 70°F (21°C), but this is not absolutely necessary. Healthy, flowering plants can be grown in a range from 60°F to 80°F (16-29°C). Any temperatures higher or lower could result in a lack of flowers and endanger the health of the plant. African violets cannot tolerate prolonged temperatures below 50°F (10°C).

Generally, daytime temperatures of 72°F to 75°F (22-24°C) are recommended for African violets with solid green foliage. Night temperatures should be around 65°F (19°C). Variegated hybrids develop more desirable leaf color with temperatures under 70°F (21°C). This is due to the fact that plants absorb more nitrogen in warmer weather and nitrogen is responsible for the production of green plant tissue.

In addition to the correct light and temperature requirements, African violets need a well-ventilated growing area. Direct air currents from open windows, however, can be just as harmful as stagnant air. The answer to this problem is usually indirect ventilation from an open window in an adjoining room.

While African violets are strictly indoor plants, other members of the gesneriad family can be summered outdoors.

Artificial light

Fluorescent light

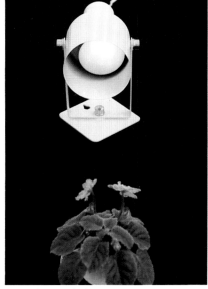

Incandescent light

Fluorescent shelf unit

With the use of artificial light, African violets can be grown anywhere in your house. In fact, African violets are generally more successful under artificial light because it is more predictable than sunlight. The constant intensity contributes to symmetrical growth.

The closer a light source duplicates the wavelengths of natural light, the better the plant will respond. Research has indicated that plants use primarily the red and blue wavelengths of the light spectrum. Red light encourages vegetative growth, while blue light regulates the respiratory system of the plant.

The popular choice for indoor gardening has become the fluorescent tube, specially modified to provide the proper balance of radiant energy. These lights also stay cool and will not scorch plants when used properly.

The basic fluorescent unit consists of a tube fixture and a reflector. Two-tube fixtures are generally preferred because they are more efficient than a single tube. The tubes vary in length from two feet to eight feet. Select the longest tube your growing space will allow.

Specially designed incandescent bulbs usually generate too much heat to be satisfactory for African violets. But some growers believe that bulbs of low wattage can stimulate plant growth. One advantage to bulbs is that they are compatible with the lamp sockets in your house.

Once your plants are under artificial lights, you have greater control over their lighting needs. Your African violets should grow at a fairly constant rate and may reward you with almost continuous bloom.

Culture under artificial lights includes more water and more nutrients on a regular schedule. The exact amounts depend on the size and porosity of the container. Temperature and humidity requirements are the same as plants grown in natural light.

The distance from the fluorescent light to the plant is based on the type of light and the maturity of the African violet. An ordinary fluorescent tube should be between six to 12 inches from the top of a mature plant. A good distance from special plant growth tubes is about 10 inches. Newly sown seeds can be started as close as four inches and then gradually moved to six to eight inches as they grow.

African violets with dark foliage should be placed near the center of the tubes where the light is more intense. Conversely, group plants with variegated foliage or light-colored flowers around the outer edges.

Under normal conditions, African violets need 10 to 12 hours of artificial light per day. To avoid overheating, this time can be reduced to as few as eight hours during hot weather. Never leave the lights on continuously. Too much light results in plants with bunched centers.

Soil and fertilizer

Components of African violet soil

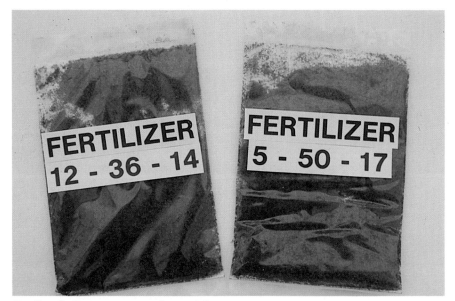

Fertilizer listing percentages of essential nutrients

African violets have very fine roots. The soil, therefore, should be light porous and provide good drainage. There are many commercial African violet potting mixes available at garden centers. They usually consist of several components.

Peat moss and leaf mold increase the water-holding capacity and help prevent nutrients from being leached away. They also permit the roots to deeply penetrate the soil in search of moisture and minerals. Perlite and vermiculite are added to lighten the soil and prevent moisture from being retained long enough to harm the roots. The tiny holes in perlite also help to store air and food that can be used by the plant as needed. Nitrohumus supplies trace elements required for nourishment. Charcoal is placed in the bottom of terrariums and containers without drain holes to keep the soil from souring.

The planting medium should be slightly acid, with a pH range of 6.5 to 6.9. Too much acid, however, will cause the plant to weaken. Occasionally, small amounts of lime are added to minimize the risk of acid build-up.

Veteran African violet growers often mix their own formulas. Beginners, however, should start with a commercial potting mix sterilized to protect against bacteria and insects.

Modern African violet potting mixes often contain no soil and few nutrients. Since the available nutrients are gradually depleted as the plant grows, you must periodically replenish the proper amounts of nitrogen, phosphorus and potassium. The percentage of these elements is indicated on commercial fertilizer containers by three numbers — nitrogen is listed first, followed by phosphorus and potassium.

The specific mineral requirements depend on whether the plant is growing or blooming. Young African violets require nitrogen to stimulate leaf and stem strength. A fertilizer in which the first number is higher than, or the same as, the other two numbers is good for this purpose. Fish emulsion with a rating of 20-20-20 is a good choice. As African violets approach the blooming stage, they will need a fertilizer lower in nitrogen and higher in phosphorus. Such a fertilizer will have a formula around 12-36-14. Variegated foliage will turn green if too much nitrogen is used. A fertilizer recommended for variegated growth is 5-50-17.

Slow-release granules or pellets are applied dry on the soil surface. A small quantity of nutrients is released each time the plant is watered. Used as directed, a single application can last up to six months. Liquid fertilizers and water-soluble powders are diluted with tepid water and can be applied at every watering or monthly to moist soil.

Water and humidity

Top watering

Bottom watering

Wick watering

Pebble tray for humidity

Three popular ways to water African violets are top watering, bottom watering and wicking.

Whichever method you select, be sure that the water is at room temperature or just a little warmer. The shock of cold water causes leaf spotting and a suppression of bloom. Tap water is fine, but beware of harmful chemicals in water that has been artificially softened with sodium or water that is too hard or alkaline. These dangers can be avoided by using rainwater or distilled water.

A long-spouted watering can is recommended for top watering. You can easily water all corners of the soil and direct moisture away from the foliage and the crown. Occasional water on either is safe, but a constantly wet crown can develop crown rot. Apply water in a gentle flow until the soil is thoroughly moistened. Allow excess water to drain away so it will not be reabsorbed from the bottom.

In bottom watering, the pot is set in a saucer of tepid water until the top of the soil becomes damp. The excess water is then discarded. Continual bottom watering leads to an accumulation of harmful mineral salts on the soil surface. It is necessary to top water periodically to flush away these salts.

You should water only when the top of the soil is dry to the touch.

A wick pot takes the guesswork out of when and how much to water your African violets. It consists of a water reservoir with a pot on top. The water is taken up into the soil by means of a fiberglass or nylon wick. Wick pots are sold commercially, or you can make your own.

A half-pound margarine tub or cheese container with a lid makes a good reservoir. The clear plastic ones allow you to see when refilling is needed. A wick, made from a four-inch strip of nylon stocking, is pulled through the drain hole and unraveled to cover the bottom of the pot. Fill the pot with damp soil. Extra perlite may have to be added to insure a porous consistency. Thoroughly water the plant from the top, then feed the wick through a hole cut in the lid of the reservoir. Another hole, near the edge of the lid, will make refilling easier. Your wick pot should provide water for up to two weeks. Water from the top about once a month to leach away the accumulated mineral salts.

In addition to water in the soil, African violets require adequate amounts of water in the air in order to bloom. The preferred humidity range of 40 to 60 percent can generally be found in any kitchen or bathroom. The proper humidity can also be maintained by grouping plants together on shallow trays filled with porous lava rock and water. Misting the foliage is beneficial, as long as the water is of room temperature.

Containers

Variety of containers

Novelty container

Uncovered terrarium

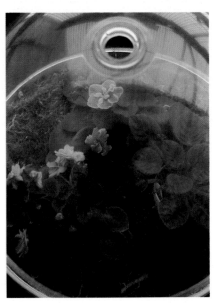

Covered terrarium

Not every type of container is suitable for African violets. Several important factors should be considered before you select from among the many containers currently on the market.

Unglazed clay pots were popular a number of years ago. Water evaporation through the sides and good aeration of the soil are two advantages, especially for people who tend to overwater. But clay also dries out fast and the rim slowly becomes coated with fertilizer salts from the evaporation.

Plastic pots are preferred for their ability to keep moisture and temperature at uniform levels. They come in many colors, are lightweight and easy to clean. One disadvantage is that plastic pots hold water longer than clay. This can lead to crown rot if the soil remains soggy over a prolonged period.

Whichever type of pot you select, make sure it has a drain hole in the bottom. Some decorative glazed pots do not have this necessary feature. You can still grow your African violet in a favorite glazed pot or novelty container by simply setting a properly potted plant inside of it, instead of potting directly into the soil of a drainless container.

African violets prefer to be slightly rootbound. It is a good idea to use the smallest size pot that will accomodate the root system of your plant.

Terrariums and miniature African violets seem to be made for each other. The enclosed environment provides the ideal moisture and humidity, and the plants are small enough that they won't rapidly outgrow the container. Certain small and tender gesneriads are also good terrarium subjects.

Terrariums can be made from any transparent container that is at least eight inches across. Anything smaller usually appears to cramp the plants. Bowls, jars, bottles, aquariums and brandy snifters have all been successfully adapted as terrariums. Make sure they are deep enough for a few inches of soil and have an opening large enough for planting and maintaining.

In the bottom of the container, place a one-inch layer of charcoal and gravel. Add enough sphagnum moss to cover the drainage material and place at least three inches of soil on top. Lower your plant in position and carefully firm the soil around the roots.

Water requirements will depend on whether the terrarium is covered or uncovered. Keep the soil moderately moist, not soggy. Also avoid direct sunlight which can burn delicate foliage. If your plants are growing well, there is no need to fertilize. (For additional information see "Terrariums & Other Nice Things" HP-419 by Gick Publishing Inc.)

Transplanting

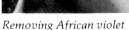
Removing African violet

Preparing soil in new container

Loosening old soil

Tamping down soil

Unlike many houseplants, African violets should not be transplanted every time they appear too large for their containers. In fact, placing them in too large a pot can actually be fatal. Overpotting usually results in overwatering. This reduces the amount of air in the soil and causes damage to the roots. To prevent this, develop a tendency to keep the plant in a small, squatty pot.

You should repot when the plant is obviously top heavy or when the soil dries out very frequently. Excessive dryness could also mean the soil is old. In this case, transplant to the same size pot.

Before transplanting, make sure all containers are clean. For containers with large drain holes, place a curved piece of broken pot over the opening and cover with additional pieces to prevent loss of soil. For pots with small or no drain holes, provide a bottom layer of perlite and charcoal where excess water may accumulate.

Because the foliage is so brittle, African violets must be transplanted gently. Fortunately, most African violets are sold in plastic pots. You can easily loosen moist soil by squeezing the sides of the pot. Forcing a pencil through the drain hole should free the more stubborn root balls. With two fingers under the leaves and around the soil, tip the pot to the side and ease the plant from its container.

One method of preparing the soil in the new container, is to create a mold with a pot the same size as the one in which your plant has been growing. Place this pot over the drainage material and firm the potting mix around it. Twist the pot and remove it. Before you place the plant in this depression, loosen the old soil around the root ball and remove any charcoal that is still clinging to it. Position the plant deep enough to allow at least a half inch space for watering. Settle the soil by tapping the pot on a hard surface, then lightly tamp it down with your fingers.

The transplanting process may leave the leaves somewhat soiled. If allowed to remain, this could eventually reduce the amount of light the plant receives. A soft bristled brush will remove most dirt and dust.

The newly-potted plant should be thoroughly watered. Either soak the soil from the top and let it drain, or place the pot in a pan of water until the surface of the soil is moist. Allow the excess water to drain before setting the plant in an area away from direct sun. After a few weeks of moderate watering, move your plant to its permanent location.

Some fast growing African violets may appear to grow out of their pots if they are not replanted soon enough. A neck will form above the soil line where the old leaves have been removed. This neck will develop roots when it is repotted up the lower leaves.

Hybridizing

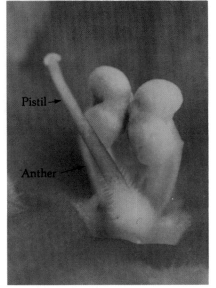

Reproductive organs

Removing anther from pollen parent

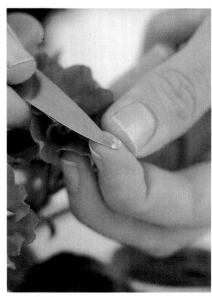

Splitting anther

Applying pollen to seed parent

Hybridizing is the breeding or cross-pollinating of different varieties or species. The plants grown from the resulting seeds will possess characteristics of the parent plants according to complex genetic principles.

Both the male and female elements necessary for pollination are visible on a single flower. The yellow center is composed of pollen sacs called *anthers.* The small, protuding spike is the pollen-receiving tube called a *pistil.* Actually, the pistil consists of three parts. The tube itself is the style. *The ovary* is located beneath the flower and contains the immature seeds. When pollen is placed on the *stigma* at the tip of the style, the fertilization process has begun.

Cross-pollination is as simple as transferring the pollen from the anther of one flower to the stigma of another. One method is to cut the anther from one flower with a knife. With the clean knife point, slit the pollen sac open. Allow the dust-like pollen grains to fall on the blade and touch it to the stigma of the other flower. You can also bring the open sac in direct contact with the stigma. Best results are obtained with mature flowers when the stigma becomes slightly sticky.

Write the date and the names of plants crossed on a marker in waterproof ink. List the seed parent first, followed by an "X" and the name of the pollen parent. Place this marker in the container of the seed parent.

If fertilization has taken place, the seedpod will ripen in six to nine months. Wait until the seed capsule turns brown and begins to shrivel before removing it. Place it in a warm spot to dry. The seeds will be ready for sowing in two to three weeks.

As your hybrid seedlings come into flower, compare their characteristics with those of the parents. The colors and shapes of the flowers and leaves will most resemble the seed parent. The traits that occur most often are called *dominant,* the others are called *recessive.* Blue, for instance, is a dominant color.

Occasionally, due to a change in the genetic structure, the chromosome count will double. The resulting plant, with heavy-textured foliage and large flowers, is called a "Supreme." In an even rarer occurance, a seed will produce a variation that never existed before. A mutation occurs maybe once in a hundred-thousand plants. To determine if the new characteristic is stable, the plant is propagated by leaf cuttings for three generations.

The variety of color and form of flowers and foliage you see in the African Violet Album section bears testimony to the dedication of the hybridizer. It is even more amazing when you consider that most of these varieties were derived from just two or three original species.

Propagation

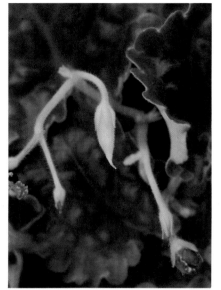
Ripening seed pod

Young African violet seedlings

Removing sucker

Planting sucker

African violets can be propagated in many ways. Watching them grow from seeds can be a fascinating experience, especially if the seeds are from your own hybrid crosses. Seeds are also available from some commercial growers. These seeds should be sown soon after purchase, while seeds from ripe pods can wait two to three weeks before sowing.

African violet seeds can be grown in any shallow container that can hold a rooting medium and be covered. An ordinary flower pot and a sheet of plastic will work nicely. The sowing medium should be light and well-drained. Sterilized vermiculite is easy and effective.

After filling the container with barely damp starting mix, lightly scatter the seeds over the surface. Cover the pot and put it in a bright place where the temperatures range from 75° to 80°F (24°-27°C).

The seeds should germinate in two to four weeks. During this time, keep the seeds covered and the mix damp, but not soggy. When the seedlings appear, place in a cooler spot. Seedlings are ready to transplant when they are half an inch tall. Use a tooth pick or nail file to lift out each seedling, allowing part of the soil to remain on the roots. Pot each seedling in a 2¼-inch pot filled with equal parts starting mix and regular African violet soil. Give the seedlings good light, but no direct sun. As they become established, they will require the care of mature plants.

Suckers are growing points or young crowns other than the central crown. If allowed to grow, they could develop a crowded, distorted, multiple-crowned plant. Florists sell multiple-crowned plants because they produce a better single profusion of blooms. These plants, however, are grown in a forced greenhouse environment which is difficult to maintain under home conditions. Today's hybrids, therefore, will grow and bloom better as houseplants if the suckers are removed.

Once the suckers are removed, they become another source of plants. When it grows big enough to handle, separate the sucker from the main plant with a sharp instrument. Plant it in a 2½-inch pot filled with equal parts of potting mix and vermiculite. Cover with a plastic bag. After three weeks, partially uncover the plant. Remove the bag entirely after a few more days. This will minimize the effects of shock.

If you have a multiple-crowned plant that gets too large for its pot, you can divide the crowns into a number of smaller individual plants. First, remove the plant from the pot and examine the growth of the leaves. You should notice separate clumps. Carefully, pull these apart so that you get part of the crown core with each section. Plant them in 2¼-inch pots filled with fresh potting mix. Water sparingly and keep out of direct sun for a few weeks.

Propagation

Trimming leaf stem on a slant

Rooting leaf in water

Rooting leaf in vermiculite

Stages of root and plantlet development

In addition to dividing crowns, planting suckers and sowing seeds, you can increase your collection of African violets by rooting leaves in water or soil.

Firm, healthy leaves propagate the best. Select one about halfway from the center of the plant. In other words, it should not be an old leaf, nor should it be a young leaf. With a sharp knife or razor blade, remove the leaf with about two inches of stem and trim the end on a slant.

To root the leaf in water, fill a glass with water and cap it with aluminum foil or wax paper secured with a rubber band. Make a slit in the paper and insert the stem or stems. (It is possible to root several leaves in a single glass). Place the glass in a cool, humid location. A bright, but not sunny, kitchen window is a good spot. Maintain the water level by adding water as needed.

Roots will form in two to four weeks. When the roots are about half an inch long, gently transfer the leaf to a two-inch pot filled with moistened planter mix.

Leaves can also be rooted in a bowl of pebbles. Fill a bowl with pebbles, a few charcoal chips and add water. Keeping the leaves away from the water, place the ends of the stems in the bowl. Transfer to soil when the leaves of the young plantlets are one inch long.

Leaves started directly in African violet potting mix are slower to develop roots, but there is less danger of harming them due to transplanting. The ends of the stems are trimmed on a slant and may be dusted with a rooting hormone.

A single leaf can be rooted in a 2¼-inch pot filled with a mixture of moistened potting soil and vermiculite. Insert the stem deep enough so it will be supported by the soil mixture. To avoid decay, do not permit the leaf to rest on the soil surface. Prop up the leaf with toothpicks if necessary. Best results are obtained when the pot is covered. A drinking glass or a plastic bag will provide a miniature greenhouse environment. Remove the cover temporarily if you see excess moisture on the sides.

Place the pot in a bright spot, away from direct sunlight. As long as the soil remains slightly moist, there is no need to water. Roots should form in two to five weeks. When the plantlets appear, some people recommend cutting the "mother" leaf to provide additional energy for the growing plants. The new plants should be ready for transplanting to individual pots in about 20 weeks when they are two inches tall.

You will find several groups of plantlets attached at the base of the mother leaf. They are easily separated. Transplant each plant to a two-inch pot filled with moistened potting mix.

Other Gesneriads

Photograph courtesy of Mel Sater, St. Paul, MN

Nematanthus 'Tropicana'

Photograph courtesy of Mel Sater, St. Paul, MN

Kohleria 'Connecticut Belle'

Photograph courtesy of Joan Franson, Denver, CO

Streptocarpus kirkii

Photograph courtesy of Frances Batcheller, NH

Paradrymonia ciliosa

There are a number of plants in the same family as African violets that are every bit as lovely and are just as easy to grow. As companions to your African violet, you can select large and small, upright or trailing varieties with flowers in the shapes of trumpets, cups, stars and discs in every color from gentle whites to shocking reds.

Gesneriads can be divided into three categories based on their root systems. There are those with tubers, those with rhizomes and those with fibrous roots. Knowing which category a particular plant is in can tell you something about its growth characteristics and how it may be propagated.

A tuber is a short, fleshy stem that stores food and allows a plant to survive adverse conditions in the wild. Plants with tubers have a pronounced rest period when all foliage dies away. You should gradually decrease watering and fertilizing. Store the dormant tubers in their original pots or in vermiculite in a cool, dry place. Mist occasionally to prevent the tubers from drying out completely. When the new growth starts in a few months, repot in fresh soil with the indented side of the tuber facing up. Gradually return to regular watering and fertilizing. The most commonly available tuberous gesneriads are *sinningias*.

You can propagate large tubers by cutting them into pieces and dusting them with a fungicide. Make sure each piece has at least one growth eye.

Rhizomes are horizontal stems anchored by roots. Gesneriad rhizomes are scaly and grow underground. They are capable of supporting the plant during the dry season in the wild and can withstand a wider range of temperatures and light than other gesneriads. A dormancy period is brought on by short days and dry soil. When this happens, you should store them in a cool place, water less and withhold all fertilizer. Repot and return to regular culture in the spring.

Smithiantha, gloxinia, kohleria and others with scaly rhizomes can be propagated by breaking the rhizomes apart and placing them in a rooting medium.

The greatest number of gesneriads have fibrous roots. After a heavy flowering season, these plants signal their dormancy in several ways. *Episcias* drop their lower leaves and stop all new growth. *Columnea* and *streptocarpus* just tend to look shabby. Gradually decrease applications of water and fertilizer. When the plants show signs of new growth, resume normal culture.

Plants with fibrous roots can be propagated by seeds or cuttings.

Miniatures and trailers

Two African violet miniatures

Trailing African violet

While most of the commonly available African violets are of the "standard" growth habit of over eight inches across, other sizes and forms are available. "Miniatures," "semi-miniatures" and "trailers" are not immature standards, they have all been specifically hybridized.

Miniature African violets look just like their standard counterparts, but they do not grow larger than six to eight inches across at maturity. They have correspondingly small leaves and flowers. Other plants that are slightly larger than miniatures, but have standard-size flowers, are known as semi-miniatures.

Because more of these plants can be grouped together in a given area, they are becoming popular with apartment dwellers and window sill gardeners. Miniatures and semi-miniatures respond to the same culture as the standard varieties, but a few adjustments are necessary because of their size.

To maintain a healthy root system and promote bloom, these plants must be kept in tiny pots. Miniatures should be grown in 2½-inch pots. Semi-miniatures should occupy no more than 3-inch pots. Due to the size of the pots, frequent watering is needed. To avoid overwatering, apply tepid water only when the soil is dry to the touch. A weak solution of fertilizer can be applied with every watering.

Good plant growth and flower abundance depends on sufficient humidity. For this reason, you will often find miniatures thriving in terrariums or snifters. Other ways of providing humidity are misting the leaves with a light spray of distilled water or placing the pots on pebble trays filled with water. Be sure to keep misted plants away from direct sun to prevent sunburn.

Miniatures grow well under fluorescent lights. You may have to place them on inverted pots so they come within the recommended six to ten inches of the light. If grown in natural light, be sure to turn the pot periodically to promote even growth.

Another variation from the rosette growth habit of standards, is a hybrid that hangs or trails over the edge of the pot. Most of these plants are related to the naturally trailing species *Saintpaulia grotei.*

Trailers grow from seven to 15 inches across. They do not grow in a vine-like manner, but rather have a hanging stalk that permits them to display foliage and flowers away from the confines of the pot. Some of these stalks may be as much as five inches in length. All trailers have medium size flowers which are very profuse when properly grown. Some of the most beautiful trailers are grown as multiple-crown plants.

Pests and sick plants

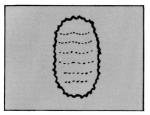

MEALY BUG: These white, fuzzy insects can be found on the undersides of leaves, lodged in the crown, or in the soil, feeding on sap.
WHAT TO DO: Isolate. Dip a cotton swab in rubbing alcohol and wipe them off the stems and leaves. Use malathion for soil mealy bugs.

APHIDS: These are green, red or black soft-bodied insects. Accumulating primarily on new growth, they suck out vital plant juices.
WHAT TO DO: Isolate. Wash off with lukewarm water. Use a malathion spray for heavier infestations.

THRIPS: These microscopic insects are usually noticed only after the damage is done. They cause leaf curl, bud drop and mottled flowers.
WHAT TO DO: Isolate. Remove flowers and buds. Use a malathion spray for heavier infestations.

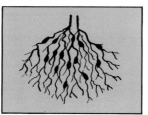

NEMATODES: Tiny soil worms that cause plants to droop and turn greenish yellow. Remove the plant and check for swollen roots.
WHAT TO DO: Nematocides are available, but the safest remedy is to destroy the infested plant. Prevent by using sterilized potting soil.

In addition to the common pests pictured above, African violets and gesneriads are subject to attacks by several kinds of mites. Cyclamen mites are particularly troublesome because they cannot be seen with the naked eye. You become aware of their presence through unusually hairy foliage, stunted growth, streaked flowers and leaves that curl up. A leaf that curls down is evidence of broad mites. Red spider mites will leave cobwebs on foliage and flowers. Since these pests travel by contact, the first thing you should do is isolate the infested plant. Then treat it with a spray solution of malathion.

Most problems with pests can be prevented if you use only sterilized potting soil, isolate all new plants for at least two weeks and inspect frequently for signs of damage. You will find, however, that quite a few problems are simply the result of poor growing practices.

The most common cultural faults are associated with watering and fertilizing. Overwatering tends to compact the soil which deprives the roots of air and turns the leaves yellow. Constantly soggy soil and watering the center of the plant can lead to crown rot. This fungus disease causes a plant to go limp. The plant can usually be saved by taking it out of the pot, removing the old soil and dead roots, and re-potting it in fresh, well-drained soil.

Wilted, burned or curled leaves can be caused by an accumulation of fertilizer salts on the surface of the soil or on the rims of clay pots. A stem injured in this way invites infection from fungi and bacteria. The best way to prevent this is to periodically water from the top.

Insufficient fertilizing results in yellow leaves, small growth and flowers that are smaller than usual. This problem can be corrected by fertilizing more often. Too much fertilizer will produce dark green leaves, but few flowers. In this case, fertilize less often with a low-nitrogen fertilizer.

Weak, leggy growth and the production of very few flowers could be due to insufficient light. You can improve this situation by moving the plant to a well-lighted window or by using artificial lights. Plants suffering from too much light will have bleached and curled foliage. Place these plants away from direct sunlight.

Leaves with dull brown edges and flowers that are smaller than normal could be the victims of insufficient humidity. The remedy is to place pots in trays filled with pebbles and water. Excessive humidity and cool temperatures can encourage botrytis blight. This is a gray mold that rots the center leaves. You can correct this problem by removing the infected tissue and applying a fungicide.

Jane Starr

African Violet Album

This section is designed to familiarize you with the multitude of African violets available. The plants shown are widely varied and are representative of many different characteristics. All the hybrid names are listed alphabetically, without regard to growth habit. Technically, the names should be preceded by the genus name of *Saintpaulia*.

The description with each plant includes the shape and color of the flower, the type of foliage and the growth habit.

Varieties described as "standard" are those that grow over 12 inches across. A large standard will grow up to 18 inches across, while a small standard will grow from 10 to 12 inches across.

"Miniatures" are usually six inches across or smaller. "Semi-miniatures" will grow up to eight inches across.

Plants listed as "Supremes" are mutations of varieties whose chromosome count has doubled. Their foliage is heavy and brittle and their flowers are larger than normal.

The name in parentheses is the person or persons who hybridized that particular plant. Varieties marked with an asterisk (*) have been registered with the African Violet Society of America. This usually indicates that these plants are of "show quality."

AFTER DARK*
(Richter)
Dark purple double flowers. Quilted, ovate foliage. Standard type.

ALICE MARIE
(Volkmann)
Creamy-pink double flowers. Tailored, serrated edged foliage. Standard type.

ATLANTIS
(Granger G.)
Ruffled double white flower with blue edging. Light green slightly wavy foliage. Standard type.

BABY DEAR*
(Lyon)
Full double white star flower. Sometimes has a trace of pink. Plain, pointed foliage. Miniature type.

BLUE HALO
(Granger G.)
Double blue-lavender flower with a white edge. Ruffled, dark green foliage. Standard type.

BLIZZARD SUPREME
(Parker)
Large white double flower. Supreme type foliage, medium size grower.

CABARET*
(Granger G.)
Double dark red flower with white fringed edge. Quilted, wavy foliage. Standard type.

BLUE EXCITEMENT*
(C. Wilson)
Medium blue double flower with bright yellow stamens. Plain, quilted, pointed foilage with serrated edge. Large type.

CALIFORNIA SKIES*
(C. Wilson)
Double dark rose flower with fringed white edge. Quilted, ruffled, fringed pointed foliage. Standard type.

CALIFORNIA SUNRISE*
(C. Wilson)
Double fringed, fuchsia-red flower with white edge. Ruffled foliage. Standard type.

CASHMERE PINK
(M. Lanigan)
Bright pink, ruffled double flower. Slightly wavy, serrated foliage. Standard type.

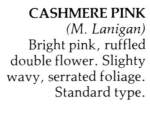

CAPRI
(Volkmann)
Semi-double Fuchsia star flower. Medium green leaves. Standard type.

CHRISTIE LOVE
(Lyon)
Double coral flowers. Nearly black-red backed foliage. Standard type.

CAROL*
(Max Maas)
Double frilled, lavender-pink flower. Quilted, ruffled foliage. Standard type.

CINDERELLA'S SLIPPER*
(Hammond)
Red-violet two-tone flowers. Spooned shape leaves. Semi-miniature type.

CINDY
(Naomi)
Double ruffled, medium peach pink flowers. Variegated "girl" leaves. Standard type.

CRADLE SONG
(E. Fisher)
Single to semi-double heliotrope star flower with white edge. Tailored leaves. Miniature type.

CORAL CAPER*
(Lyon)
Double reddish-violet star flowers. Plain foliage. Standard type.

CRUNCHER
(Lyon)
Double purple-blue flower. Dark "girl" foliage. Semi-miniature type.

CORAL CASCADE*
(Lyon)
Single reddish-pink flower with darker center. Plain foliage. Standard type.

DAINTY DOLL
(Granger G.)
Light blue star flower with wide white edge. Ruffled foliage. Standard type.

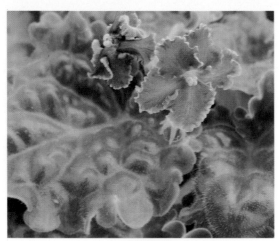

DEBBIE
(Granger G.)
Single white and purple flower. Light ruffled foliage. Standard type.

DUET
(Richter)
Bright blue, double flower with white edge. Dark tailored foliage. Standard type.

DOUBLE TAKE*
(Lyon)
Double pansy, purple star flower. Quilted, ovate foliage. Miniature type.

ELISA FREW*
(E. Fisher)
Double rosy-fuchsia star flower. Plain, quilted, glossy foliage. Standard type.

DREAM WEAVER
(Lyon)
Large semi-doubled, dark fuchsia star flowers. Dark tailored foliage. Standard type.

EL TORO SUPREME
(Kahler, supremed by C. Wilson)
Variable full double flower. May vary from bright pink to white with green edge. Standard type.

FAITH*
(Granger G.)
Double fringed, pure white flower. Quilted, ovate, pointed foliage. Standard type.

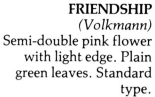

FRIENDSHIP
(Volkmann)
Semi-double pink flower with light edge. Plain green leaves. Standard type.

FLAMINGO*
(Max Maas)
Double ruffled deep rosy-pink flower. Plain foliage. Standard type.

GARNET ELF*
(Granger G.)
Fringed dark rose-lavender single flower with broad white border. Ruffled foliage. Standard type.

FREEDOM TRAIL
(Lyon)
Double fuchsia flower. Dark flexible trailer foliage. Standard type.

GARNET ELF SPORT
(Granger G.)
Sport of "Garnet Elf". Fringed white star flower. Ruffled foliage with serrated edge. Standard type.

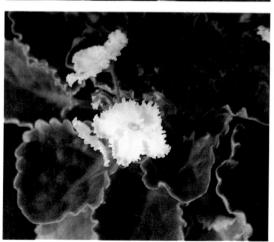

GRANGER'S BANDMASTER*
(Granger G.)
Deep red double flower, wavy star with white edge. Ruffled foliage. Standard type.

GRANGER'S BLUE TEMPEST*
(Granger G.)
Double light blue flower. Plain, spooned, pointed foliage. Standard type.

GRANGER'S BLUE BELLE*
(Granger G.)
Double fringe, medium blue flower. Plain, quilted foliage. Standard type.

GRANGER'S CAMEO QUEEN*
(Granger G.)
Double buff-white flower. Very dark olive green, plain, quilted foliage. Standard type.

GRANGER'S BLUE REGENT*
(Granger G.)
Double deep purple flower, wavy star with white edge. Plain, quilted foliage. Standard type.

GRANGER'S FESTIVAL*
(Granger G.)
Double white fringed star flower with broad red band edge. Ruffled variegated foliage. Standard type.

GRANGER'S LILAC TIME*
(Granger G.)
Double fringed, light lavender flower. Plain, quilted, pointed foliage. Standard type.

GRANGER'S PINKS-A-POPPIN*
(Granger G.)
Double deep pink flower. Quilted "girl" foliage. Standard type.

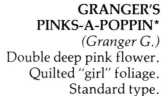

GRANGER'S PEACH FROST*
(Granger G.)
Full double ivory-peach flower. Upper petal copper tipped. Plain, quilted, pointed foliage. Large type.

GRANGER'S ROSE FROST*
(Granger G.)
Fringed double white flower with a thin red ruffle. Strawberry ruffled variegated foliage. Standard type.

GRANGER'S PINK SWAN*
(Granger G.)
Double light shell-pink flower. Plain, pointed foliage. Standard type.

GRANGER'S SERENITY*
(Granger G.)
Double fringed white and dark purple flower with ruffled edge. Ruffled foliage. Standard type.

GRANGER'S SWISS BALLET*
(Granger G.)
Single fringed white flower with blue edge. Quilted, ruffled foliage. Standard type.

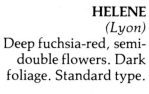

HELENE
(Lyon)
Deep fuchsia-red, semi-double flowers. Dark foliage. Standard type.

GRANGER'S WILDFIRE*
(Granger G.)
Double fringed red-violet flower with a white edge. Plain, quilted, pointed foliage. Standard type.

INDEPENDENCE
(Lyon)
Double red-violet flowers. Dark green, red backed foliage. Standard type.

GYPSY TRAIL
(Lyon)
Full double rose-pink flowers. Plain foliage. Trailer type.

JET TRAIL
(Lyon)
Full double wisteria-blue flower. Plain, pointed foliage. Semi-trailer type.

JIM DANDY
(Lyon)
Double dark blue flower with deeper lavender shading. Plain, quilted foliage. Standard type.

LAVENDER TEMPEST*
(Granger G.)
Double fringed lavender-pink flower with red petal tipping. Plain, quilted, pointed foliage. Standard type.

JOHN PAUL
(E. Fisher)
Semi-double deep royal blue fringe star flower. Medium green, semi-wavy foliage. Standard type.

LEILA*
(Max Maas)
Double white flower with green on the upper petals marked with purple. Quilted pointed foliage with ruffled edges. Standard type.

LAVENDER SPICE*
(Granger G.)
Double light lavender flower with red-lavender petal edge. Quilted, pointed foliage. Standard type.

LIKE WOW SPORT
(Lyon)
Giant royal purple flowers, semi-double. Flowers are mottled with white in sport. Ruffled, quilted leaves. Standard type.

LILI ROSA*
(Lifebore)
Two-tone dark red flower. Plain, quilted, supreme foliage. Large type.

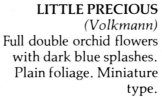

LITTLE PRECIOUS
(Volkmann)
Full double orchid flowers with dark blue splashes. Plain foliage. Miniature type.

LITTLE JIM*
(Max Maas)
Double medium pink flower. Plain, pointed foliage. Semi-miniature type.

LITTLE RASCAL
(Lyon)
Double deep purple star flower with white edge and markings. Dark green foliage. Miniature type.

LITTLE LULU
(Lyon)
Full double rosy-pink flower. Variegated foliage with red back. Semi-miniature type.

LITTLE RED
(Max Maas)
Single red flower. Dark quilted foliage. Miniature type.

LORA LOU
(Lyon)
Double to semi-double rosy-pink flower. Variegated, quilted, dark green leaves. Semi-miniature trailing type.

MARK E.*
(M. Lanigan)
Medium blue semi-double flowers edged in white. Tailored, quilted green foliage with red back. Extremely floriferous. Standard type.

MARGARET CHRISTINE
(Fischer)
Semi-double fuchsia star flowers with white edge. Glossy strawberry foliage. Standard type.

MARY D*
(Max Maas)
Double dark red star flower. Plain tailored foliange. Standard type.

MARK*
(Max Maas)
Double fringed deep red flower. Quilted, ruffled foliage. Standard type.

MIMI
(M. Lanigan)
Double red flower with slightly deeper edge. Frilly dark foliage. Standard type.

MINI MIGNON*
(Annalee)
Double fantasy, deep
amethyst star flower.
Dark green rosette form-
ing foliage. Miniature
type.

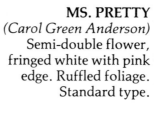

MS. PRETTY
(Carol Green Anderson)
Semi-double flower,
fringed white with pink
edge. Ruffled foliage.
Standard type.

MOHAWKS
(Granger G.)
Deep fuchsia-red semi-
double flower. Dark
green, tailored foliage.
Standard type.

MS. PRETTY PINK
(Carol Green Anderson)
Semi-double flower,
fringed pink. Ruffled
foliage. Standard type.

MONACO
(Granger G.)
White semi-double flower
with medium blue edge.
Light tailored foliage.
Standard type.

MYSTICAL BLUE
(Lyon)
Semi-double wisteria-
blue flower. Forest green
foliage. Standard type.

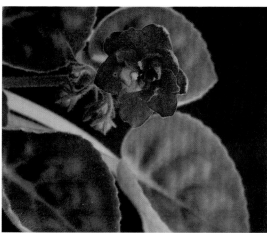

0-2
(Granger G.)
Double red flowers.
Medium green, tailored
foliage. Standard type.

PETUNIA
(Spontz)
Single white flower with
blue center. Light tailored
foliage. Semi-miniature
type.

PAT'S PET*
(Lyon)
Double green flower with
deeper green edges. Holly
foliage. Standard type.

PINK AMISS
(Granger G.)
Double dark pink flowers
with white edge. Round
foliage. Standard type.

PEPPERMINT STICK
(Lyon)
Double two-tone fuchsia
and white flowers. Scal-
loped edged leaves.
Standard type.

**PINK BLIZZARD
SUPREME**
(Parker)
Sport of "Blizzard
Supreme". Double large
pink flower. Round
supreme type foliage.
Supreme type.

PINK FLAME
(Granger G.)
Double medium pink flowers. Green quilted, tailored foliage with serrated edges. Standard type.

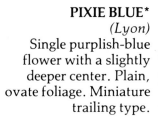

PIXIE BLUE*
(Lyon)
Single purplish-blue flower with a slightly deeper center. Plain, ovate foliage. Miniature trailing type.

PINK REGENT
(Granger G.)
Double deep pink flowers. Slightly wavy, serrated foliage. Large type.

PIXIE TRAIL
(Lyon)
Small violet shaped pink flower with deeper center. Plain, ovate foliage. Miniature trailing type.

PINK VIXEN
(Lyon)
Double frosted rose-pink flowers spotted with purple. Plain foliage. Standard type.

POCONO MOUNTAIN
(De Sandis)
Semi-double purple star flower with darker purple border trimmed in white. Tailored foliage. Standard type.

PRETTY POLLY
(Irene Fredette)
Semi-double pink star flowers with cherry-red edge. Dark strawberry foliage. Standard type.

RASPBERRY REVEL*
(Everglad)
Double raspberry flower. Quilted, pointed, ovate foliage. Standard type.

PURPLE CASCADE
(Granger G.)
Deep purple full ruffled double flower. Wavy, yellow, variegated foliage. Standard type.

RED FLAME
(Granger G.)
Semi-double deep red flower. Medium green tailored foliage. Standard type.

PURPLE NAUTILUS
(M. Lanigan)
Double frilled, very dark purple flower. Dark, glossy, wavy foliage. Standard type.

REGINA*
(Granger G.)
Double pure white flower. Occasionally one may have a lavender coloring. Plain, quilted, ovate foliage. Standard type.

ROBERTA
(Granger G.)
Semi-double flowers with frilled shades of pink-lavender. Medium green foliage with ruffled edges. Standard type.

SISTER ANCILLA
(M. Lanigan)
Single pink flower with deeper pink center. Flat, dark green foliage. Standard type.

ROSE EMBER
(Granger G.)
Double rose-pink flower with deeper color on tips. Plain, tailored foliage. Standard type.

SNOW BERRY
(Lyon)
Double vibrant pink flower with chalk white edge. Very dark glossy foliage with red back. Standard type.

SHOCKING
(Irene Fredette)
Double shocking pink flower. Showy, plain foliage. Standard type.

SNOW BUNNY
(Hammond)
Double white flower. "Girl" foliage. Miniature type.

SPICY
(Lyon)
Double pink flower
spotted with purple.
Dark green foliage.
Standard type.

SUPERBA*
(Granger G.)
Double old rose-orchid
flower with light fringe.
Quilted, ruffled foliage.
Standard type.

SPLASHES
(Lyon)
Lilac star flower splashed
with blue. Dark tailored
foliage. Standard type.

SUPERSTAR
(M. Lanigan)
Double deep fuchsia-
pink star flower with
deeper center. Tailored
foliage. Standard type.

STAR BURST
(Granger G.)
Large pink single star
flower with deeper center
and bright yellow
stamens. Serrated dark
green foliage. Standard
type.

SWEET HONESTY
(Lyon)
Frilled, bright pink double
flower. Variegated,
quilted, dark green
foliage. Standard type.

TANGIER*
(Granger G.)
Semi-double fringed red flower with a white edge. Ruffled, variegated foliage. Standard type.

TINY TEEN
(Lyon)
Full double reddish-pink flower with some white. Dark green, plain foliage. Miniature type.

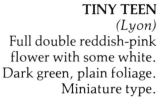

TINY ELLIE*
(Lyon)
Double rose-pink star flower. Plain, glossy foliage. Leaves are smaller than flower. Miniature type.

TOP DOLLAR*
(Rienhardt)
Double dark bluish-purple flower. Plain, variegated foliage. Standard to large type.

TINY SPARKLES*
(Lyon)
Double mauve star flower with burgundy tip, tipped with a white dot. Plain foliage. Miniature type.

TOY CLOWN
(Lyon)
Double pink flower with purple specks. Glossy foliage. Miniature type.

VENETIAN LACE*
(Granger G.)
Double white flower
with frilled orchid edge.
Quilted, ruffled foliage.
Standard type.

WILD COUNTRY*
(Lyon)
Blue-violet semi-double
flower. Dark green
foliage. Standard type.

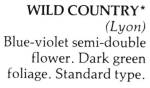

WEE LASS
(Lyon)
Double white star flower
with frilled bright fuchsia
edge. Semi-holly foliage.
Miniature type.

WILLIAM BRUCE*
E. Fisher)
Semi-double morrish-blue
flower with a deeper edge.
Plain, quilted foliage.
Large type.

WHIRLAWAY
(Lyon)
Huge purplish-blue double
star flower with white
edge. Round, quilted,
plain dark foliage.
Standard type.

WINTER GRAPE*
(Irene Fredette)
Semi-double fringed
orchid to violet flower.
Plain, variegated foliage.
Standard type.

Sinningia pusilla

Gesneriad Album

This section is designed to present a small sample of the many gesneriads available. As companions for your African violets, these plants are most appropriate as they all respond to the same general culture. The more tender of these plants are suited for a terrarium environment, while the hardier ones can be grown outdoors in sheltered patios. All plants are listed alphabetically by scientific name.

The most reliable way of referring to a gesneriad is by its scientific name. It consists of a genus (the large group to which a plant is related) and a species (the specific plant).

Some popular gesneriads are known by common names. Unfortunately, these names are not uniform throughout the world. Even in the same locality, there may be different common names for the same plant. The more permanent names are listed in double quotation marks (").

Occasionally, stable varients occur in a cultivated gesneriad. If they are of interest, these are given a name. These names appear after the scientific name and are enclosed in single quotation marks (').

The description with each plant includes the shape and color of the flower, the type and texture of the foliage, and something about the growth habit.

AESCHYNANTHUS
'Black Pagoda'
Trailing, free-blooming hybrid with orange and yellow tubular flowers. Dark green leaves, mottled with maroon.

AESCHYNANTHUS
javanicus
Called "Lipstick Plant" for its brilliant red flowers. Small green leaves are waxy with slightly toothed edges.

ALLOPLECTUS
calochlamys
Shrubby plant with narrow white-haired leaves and flowers that are pink on the outside and white on the inside.

CODONANTHE
crassifolia
Vining plant with stiff, waxy leaves and creamy-white flowers with yellow throats.

COLUMNEA
'Magic Latern"
Vining hybrid with red and yellow flowers covered with fine hairs. Green leaves are narrow and shiny.

COLUMNEA
'Blue Velvet'
Large hybrid with dark orange and yellow flowers covered with silky white hairs. Foliage is dark green.

COLUMNEA
'Orange Queen'
Tubular orange flowers give this hybrid the name "Flying Fish Plant." Leaves are narrow and bright green.

COLUMNEA gloriosa
Long stemmed, trailing plant with large red and yellow flowers. Small green to purple leaves are covered with fine hairs.

COLUMNEA 'Twiggy'
Vining hybrid with large yellow flowers. Dark green leaves have pronounced veins.

EPISCIA cupreata
Silvery leaves are edged and spotted with reddish-brown. Tubular flowers are reddish-orange.

KOHLERIA 'Rongo'
Compact hybrid with white blooms marked with magenta. Dark green leaves are red-veined beneath.

GESNERIA cuneifolia
Leaves are shiny green. Bright red and yellow flowers give it the name "Firecracker Plant."

NEMATANTHUS 'Castenet'
Hybrid with peach-colored dangling flowers. Green foliage is waxy with brick red on the reverse.

GLOXINIA sylvatica
Narrow leaves and long-lasting orange flowers. Not to be confused with the florist gloxinia (*Sinningia speciosa*).

SINNINGIA cardinalis
Heart-shaped fuzzy leaves grow in a rosette. Tubular flowers are brilliant red.

SINNINGIA 'Cindy-ella'
A miniature hybrid with large, tubular purple and white flowers.

SMITHIANTHA 'Little One'
Small hybrid with orange-red blooms. Green foliage is marked with purple mottling.

SINNINGIA pusilla
The smallest tuberous gesneriad. Lilac flowers appear throughout the year under terrarium culture.

STREPTOCARPUS 'Maassen's White'
Hybrid with clump-forming stemless leaves. Flowers are white and trumpet-shaped.

SINNINGIA speciosa
"The Florist Gloxinia" comes in a wide range of hybrids. Flowers are large and usually bell-shaped. Large, wrinkled leaves have a fuzzy coat.

STREPTOCARPUS rexii hybrid
Variety of hybrids available with long, wavy, stemless leaves and trumpet-shaped flowers in white, pink, purple, red or blue.

Glossary

Anther — the yellow, pollen-bearing sacs in the center of a flower.

Cross-pollination — pollen transferred from the anther of one plant to the stigma of another.

Crown — the central growing point on a stem.

Cutting — a piece from a parent plant which generates additional plants with the same characteristics as the parent.

Genus — a subdivision of a plant family.

Hybrid — a cross between two plants that are noticeably different.

Pistil — the seed-bearing organ that consists of the ovary, the style and the stigma.

Pollen — the sperm-bearing grains that are released from the anthers.

Species — a subdivision of a genus.

Sport — a plant with transmissible differences from the parent that are due to nature and not hybridization.

Stigma — the upper part of the pistil that receives the pollen grains.

Style — the stalk-like connection between the stigma and the ovary.

Star Burst

Millie Blair